WITHDRAWN

Senses in My World

Seeing

by Martha E. H. Rustad

Bullfrog Books

Ideas for Parents and Teachers

Bullfrog Books let children practice reading informational text at the earliest reading levels. Repetition, familiar words, and photo labels support early readers.

Before Reading

- Ask the child to think about senses. Ask: How do you see?

- Look at the picture glossary together. Read and discuss the words.

Read the Book

- "Walk" through the book and look at the photos. Let the child ask questions. Point out the photo labels.

- Read the book to the child, or have him or her read independently.

After Reading

- Prompt the child to think more. Ask: What do you see around you? How does seeing help you learn?

Bullfrog Books are published by Jump!
5357 Penn Avenue South
Minneapolis, MN 55419
www.jumplibrary.com

Library of Congress Cataloging-in-Publication Data

Rustad, Martha E. H. (Martha Elizabeth Hillman), 1975- author.
  Seeing / by Martha E.H. Rustad.
    pages cm. — (Bullfrog books)
(Senses in my world)
  Summary: "This photo-illustrated book for young readers describes how seeing works and what we learn about our surroundings through our sense of sight" — Provided by publisher.
  Audience: Ages 5-8.
  Audience: K to grade 3.
  Includes bibliographical references and index.
  ISBN 978-1-62031-116-5 (hard cover) —
  ISBN 978-1-62496-183-0 (ebook) —
  ISBN 978-1-62031-150-9 (paperback)
  1. Eye — Juvenile literature.
  2. Vision — Juvenile literature. I. Title.
QP475.7.R87 2015
612.8'4—dc23
                                    2013047820

Series Editor: Rebecca Glaser
Series Designer: Ellen Huber
Book Designer: Anna Peterson
Photo Researcher: Kurtis Kinneman

Photo Credits: All photos by Shutterstock except: Getty Images/SeanShot, 18–19, 23tr; iStock/AndreasWeber, 14 (inset); iStock/asiseeit, 10–11; iStock/RichLegg, 14–15; SuperStock/Image Source, 8–9

Printed in the United States of America at Corporate Graphics, in North Mankato, Minnesota.
6-2014
10 9 8 7 6 5 4 3 2 1

Table of Contents

How Do We See?

We use our eyes to see.

How does seeing work?

light

Light bounces
off objects.

The light goes
into the eye.

The brain
understands the
light as pictures.

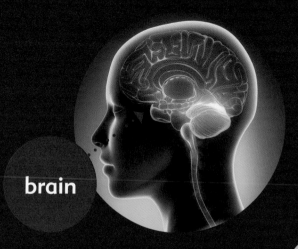

brain

What do we see?

Jess sees sunshine.

She knows it will
be warm.

Terry sees the menu.

He knows pizza is for lunch.

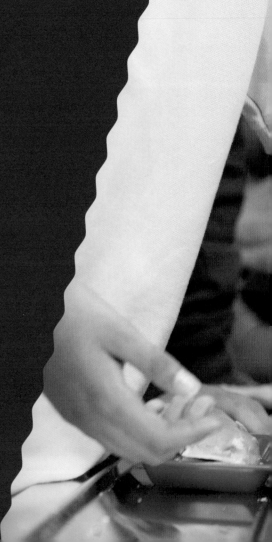

Anton sees the ball in the net. Goal!

He knows he scored.

Sam sees a green light.

He looks both ways.

He knows it is safe
to cross.

Erin sees red leaves.

She knows fall is here.

17

Will has trouble seeing.

He wears glasses.

Now he can see his book better.

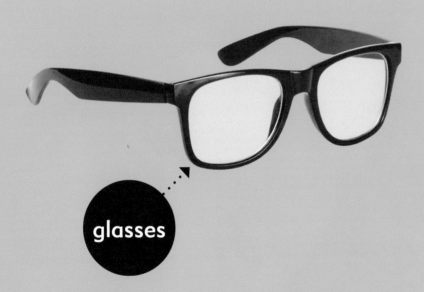

glasses

Race cars speed around a track. School buses take kids safely to school. These books tell you all about the jobs machines do. Have you read them all?

ISBN: 978-1-62031-106-6

What things do you see?
What do they tell you?

Parts of the Eye

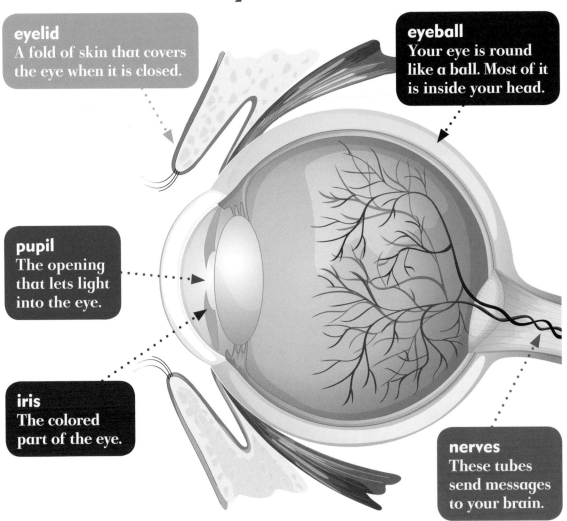

eyelid
A fold of skin that covers the eye when it is closed.

eyeball
Your eye is round like a ball. Most of it is inside your head.

pupil
The opening that lets light into the eye.

iris
The colored part of the eye.

nerves
These tubes send messages to your brain.

Picture Glossary

bounce
To hit a surface and move away from it.

glasses
Clear pieces of plastic or glass held in front of the eyes with a frame; glasses help people see.

brain
A body part in your head that helps you think and understand.

light
A brightness that lets us see.

Index

To Learn More

Learning more is as easy as 1, 2, 3.

1) Go to www.factsurfer.com

2) Enter "seeing" into the search box.

3) Click the "Surf" button to see a list of websites.

With factsurfer.com, finding more information is just a click away.